SHIRLEY CHISHOLM:

CHAMPION OF CHANGE

DR. TONYA ALLEN

Cover Artwork and Illustrations by Whimsical Designs by CJ
Design by Reyhana Ismail

All inquiries or sales request should be addressed to:

Planting People Growing Justice Press
P.O. Box 131894
Saint Paul, MN 55113
www.ppgjli.org

Printed and bound in the United States of America
First Edition
LCCN: 2024932504
1-9781959223580/9781959223610-11/1/2024

DEDICATION

This book is dedicated to my father, Charles

TABLE OF CONTENTS

Introduction
Hope for the Future 4

Chapter 1:
Born to Lead 6

Chapter 2:
Teaching for Change 8

Chapter 3:
Making a Difference in Politics 11

Chapter 4:
Creating a Pathway for the Future 19

Ways You Can Make a Difference 22

Reflection Questions 23

Author's Note 24

Author Bio 25

Quotes to Inspire 26

Glossary 29

Source Notes, Books, Websites 30

Words in **bold** are in the glossary.

BRING U.S. TOGETHER
CHISHOLM 1972
AND UNBOSSED

HOPE FOR THE FUTURE

Shirley Chisholm was determined to build a better world. This is why she was called "Fighting Shirley" because she never gave up on what she believed in. She had an unwavering commitment to the pursuit of fairness and justice. Her education provided her with the tools to advocate for change.

Shirley Chisholm was a smart young woman who started her career in the field of education. Shirley graduated from Brooklyn College in 1946 and began as a nursery aide in Harlem. Shirley continued learning and became a teacher. She graduated in 1951 from Columbia University with a master's degree in Early Childhood Education. She eventually became a childcare director at centers in Brooklyn and Manhattan.

Shirley was a leader and an educator who cared deeply about the children and families she worked with. She became an educational consultant with the Division of Day Care in New York City's Bureau of Child Welfare. Shirley's experiences led to her desire to become a greater advocate for those in need within her community, leading to her interest in politics.

P
PRESIDENT

CHAPTER 1:
BORN TO LEAD

Shirley's parents came to the United States for better jobs and housing opportunities for their family. Her father, Charles St. Hill, worked in a factory and her mother, Ruby Seale St. Hill, was a seamstress. Shirley Anita St. Hill Chisholm was born on November 30, 1924, in Brooklyn, New York. She was the oldest daughter of **immigrants** who came to the United States from Barbados.

FACT: BARBADOS

Barbados is an island nation located in the West Indies within the Caribbean.

Barbados is known for its beautiful beaches, scenic parks, and rich culture.

CHAPTER 2:
TEACHING FOR CHANGE

Shirley was born shortly before the Great Depression. This is when the United States' stock market crashed, resulting in a poor economy that left many Americans with little to nothing.

Shirley's parents needed time to recover financially, so they sent Shirley and her two younger sisters, Odessa and Muriel, to live with her grandparents in Barbados. After returning to America, Shirley's third sister, Selma, was born.

FACT: THE STOCK MARKET CRASH

The stock market crash on October 29, 1929, caused people to lose billions of dollars.

African Americans were hit hard as they were often working for companies that did not survive going into the Great Depression.

When Shirley returned to the United States, she worked hard in school. She was a smart, young woman who later graduated from Brooklyn College in 1946 at the top of her class. In addition to her grades in college, Shirley was known for her debate skills. After graduating from college, she became a teacher. In 1949, Shirley married Conrad Chisholm in 1949.

Shirley was about improving herself and returned to Columbia University where she earned a master's degree in Early Childhood Education. She transitioned from working in the classroom to being a daycare director.

In 1959, Shirley went to work for the City of New York's division of childcare as a consultant. She enjoyed her work with children, yet she wanted more. Shirley had begun to explore community activism as she wanted to see more change in her life.

Shirley knew how important it was to use her own voice. In the early 1960s, Shirley was passionate about the rights of women, rights for Black people, and ending the Vietnam War. She become involved with organizations like the National Association for the Advancement of Colored People (NAACP) and the Democratic Party club in Bedford-Stuyvesant, Brooklyn.

CHAPTER 3:
MAKING A DIFFERENCE IN POLITICS

Although education was her start, ultimately Shirley rose to the ranks of politics. One of her notable accomplishments early on was running and winning a seat in the New York State legislature in 1964. Shirley was only the second African American to win a seat.

Being seated in the New York State Legislature was not enough for Shirley. She saw the limits at the state level, and she desired even more change within her community. When court-ordered **redistricting** occurred within the district she lived, Shirley made a decision. She decided to run for a seat in the United States Congress in 1968. Shirley did not have an easy run. She had to face off in the primaries against three Black challengers. Shirley used her public speaking and debate skills to reach her community and share what she believed she could do for them that others failed to do.

When it came to the general election, Shirley faced off against James Farmer. James Farmer focused on Shirley being a woman, and he argued that Congress needed more men. But his tactic failed as Shirley campaigned on being "unbought and unbossed," Shirley became the first Black woman elected to the United States Congress, representing New York's 12th congressional district.

In politics, Shirley was known as a **congresswoman**. Getting into Congress and doing the work she campaigned she hoped to do was not easy. Shirley was determined to serve her community and remove the barriers they faced. Her goal was to make life better for children and families. She did this by lifting her voice for justice.

Shirley faced many challenges but remained unstoppable. After taking office, she was appointed to serve as a member of the Agriculture Committee. She refused to serve because animals, crops, and farming were not related to the needs of communities like her neighborhood in Brooklyn. She wanted to work on the issues that would have a positive impact right away on communities across the nation. She fought for another appointment that connected to the issues impacting those in need. She was later appointed to the Veterans' Affairs Committee. She also served on the Education and Labor Committee.

EQUAL RIGHTS AMENDMENT

On August 10, 1970, Shirley gave a passionate speech about the importance of supporting the Equal Rights Amendment. The law would provide women with the same protections and rights as men. Women were facing challenges like unfair pay and discrimination in the workplace. They were experiencing harmful working conditions that compromised their safety. They also were working longer hours without additional pay. Women also needed more access to education and training. Shirley advocated for women to attend college and develop the skills needed for better jobs.

Shirley believed everyone should be treated fairly. Hard work should lead to equal pay and more access to career advancement. Shirley fought passionately for women to achieve their dreams.

Shirley envisioned Congress meeting the needs of diverse communities. She dreamed of policies that would create equal access to jobs, education, housing, and medical care. This led her to become a founding member of the Congressional Black Caucus and National Women's Political Caucus.

Shirley was committed to training the next generation of leaders. She began by hiring and training young women to work in her office. These staff members received hands-on training in how the government operates. They also learned how to develop strategies for creating change.

Over the years, Shirley made a great impact while serving in Congress. She helped to fund daycare centers for children in need. She was concerned about hunger. Therefore, she worked to create better access to food for families. College students struggled to pay their tuition. Shirley worked to make attending college more affordable. Many families worked hard and could not afford their basic needs. She advocated for fair wages.

Shirley faced a lot of opposition due to being Black and being a woman. This experience led her to believe that she needed to be the change that no one had ever seen before. Shirley believed she could become President of the United States of America.

OUGHT
OSSED
UNBOUGHT
UNBOSSED
UNBOUGHT
UNBOSSED

In 1972, she ran for President of the United States. On January 25, 1972, she boldly declared: "I am the candidate of the people of America." She shared her vision of a better tomorrow for the entire nation. She described how the greatest potential of America was untapped. Women, communities of color, and young people had been overlooked for too long. She welcomed everyone to help build a better society together. Her words of hope filled the air. The crowd cheered as she gave her speech.

Shirley was the first woman to run for the Democratic Party's **nomination** and the first Black **candidate** to seek a major party endorsement. She was also the first woman to appear in a U.S. Presidential debate.

Shirley was not a rich woman, nor were there a lot of people who believed in her. Yet, everyday people supported her campaign by donating what they had. No amount was too small to have a great impact. Some people hosted dinners while others held block club gatherings. The coins and dollars donated continued to add up. With each donation, Fighting Shirley kept pressing forward with her campaign.

Despite many obstacles, she persisted with her campaign. Shirley had to fight and file a lawsuit to participate in debates like the other candidates. She only got to give one speech where she could be heard by a lot of potential voters. Shirley managed to participate in 12 **primary** events where she got 152 **delegates**, only 10 percent of all delegates, far short of what she needed to be the chosen candidate. Shirley did not win, yet her legacy as a fighter and a woman who broke many barriers remains to this day.

FACT: WRITING FOR JUSTICE

Shirley wrote two books about her vision for the future. In Unbought and Unbossed, she shared her journey of breaking barriers and becoming the first Black woman elected to Congress. In The Good Fight, she reflected on the leadership lessons learned while running for president.

FACT: FIRST BLACK FEMALE U.S. SENATOR

Around the time that Shirley Chisholm was graduating from high school, a woman who would eventually follow in her footsteps as a trailblazer was born.

Carol Moseley Braun was born in Chicago in 1947. Carol studied to become a lawyer and also got involved with community activism. She ran for the United States senate in 1992 and became the first female senator from Illinois and the first Black female senator in U.S. history.

Senator Braun served from 1993–1999 and ran for President in 2004. Unfortunately, she had to drop out early in the race due to the lack of financial support.

CHAPTER 4:

CREATING A PATHWAY FOR THE FUTURE

Shirley's personal life changed after her Presidential loss. She divorced Conrad Chisholm in 1977 and re-married Arthur Hardwick, Jr., a New York state legislator.

Shirley did not choose to run for President again but chose to remain in the House of Representatives until 1983 when she retired. Shirley returned to teaching, writing, and speaking. Shirley worked to help other leaders, such as Jesse Jackson, with campaigning as well. In 1991, Shirley moved to Florida. She died in Ormond Beach, Florida, on January 1, 2005. Following her death, she was awarded the **Presidential Medal of Freedom** in 2015.

Shirley was a difference maker who inspired other women, especially Black women, to raise their voices for change. Shirley did not back down or take no for an answer.

She started as an educator, and there are now several

congressional leaders who started as educators prior to entering politics.

Her legacy lives on through the efforts of people like her mentee Congresswoman Barbara Lee, who worked on Chisholm's presidential campaign and Kamala Harris, the 49th Vice President, who grew up in the shadow of Shirley's work.

FACT: THE PRESIDENTIAL MEDAL OF HONOR

The Presidential Medal of Honor was started by President Harry Truman in July 1945. President Truman created it to acknowledge people who did a significant service for the United States. It is the highest honor a non-military person can receive and has expanded to more categories for presidents to recognize people, such as artists and entertainers.

WAYS YOU CAN MAKE A DIFFERENCE

- Join the student council at your school and create change.
- Do your best in school as a student by learning as much as you can.
- Help younger students who need help with their homework.
- Speak up when you see things that are not fair.

REFLECTION QUESTIONS

- Shirley's father challenged her to focus on her studies. He stated: "Study and make something of yourself." What are your favorite subjects in school? Why do you enjoy them?

- Look around your community. What challenges is your community facing? How do you think you can help address these challenges?

- What issues do you care about? It could be something related to the environment, animal welfare, or any other topic. Why are these issues important to you?

- Leadership plays an important role in making a difference. How do you define leadership? What qualities do you think make a great leader? How are you working on developing these skills?

AUTHOR'S NOTE

How do you define a **shero**? Some people might say it means a female version of a hero, the main character in a story, or someone who saves the day. But for me, a shero is a person who inspires other people to be their own version of greatness. My shero is none other than Shirley Chisholm.

My father introduced me to Shirley Chisholm more than forty years ago when I was a little girl. My father made sure to tell me all about who Shirley Chisholm was. My father believed girls were just as capable as boys. He believed that I could do anything, just like Shirley.

Shirley was an educator and a **politician**. She was someone that no one could tell "no." No was not a part of her vocabulary. She lived to the beat of her own drum and did things her own way. Let it be known that she still remains my shero, even today.

AUTHOR BIO

Dr. Tonya Allen has worked in the field of education for more than twenty years with a focus on empowering others. She lives in Brooklyn Park, Minnesota, with her family.

QUOTES TO INSPIRE

ON LEADERSHIP:

"I'm here to tell you tonight, yes, I dare to say I'm going to run for the presidency. ... Regardless of the outcome, they will have to remember that a little hundred-pound woman, Shirley Chisholm, shook things up."

ON PERSEVERANCE:

"If they don't give you a seat at the table, bring a folding chair."

ON HERITAGE:

"Granny gave me strength, dignity and love. I learned from an early age that I was somebody. I didn't need the Black revolution to teach me that."

ON SERVICE:

"Service is the rent that you pay for room on this earth."

ON SELF-DETERMINATION:

"We must reject not only the stereotypes that others hold of us, but also the stereotypes that we hold of ourselves."

ON LEGACY:

"I am, and always will be, a catalyst for change."

ON GENDER EQUITY:

"Tremendous amounts of talent are lost to our society because that talent wears a skirt."

ON INCLUSION:

"We must reject not only the stereotypes that others hold of us, but also the stereotypes that we hold of ourselves."

ON WOMEN LEADING CHANGE:

"At present, our country needs women's idealism and determination, perhaps more in politics than anywhere else."

ON THE FUTURE:

"You don't make progress by standing on the sidelines, whimpering and complaining. You make progress by implementing ideas."

GLOSSARY

Candidate	A person who runs for a political position
Congresswoman	A female member of Congress
Delegates	A person who acts or represents another person in a political convention
Immigrant	A person who moves to another country, usually permanently
Nomination	To propose someone for election
Politician	A seeker or holder of public office
Primary	The first election to decide a candidate for a public office
Redistricting	To divide an area and create a new district for political office
Shero	A woman who is a role model for others

BOOKS

Calkhoven, Laurie. *Shirley Chishol*m. New York: Simon & Schuster, 2020.

Clinch, Shasta. *Kamala is Speaking: Vice President for the People.* New York: Random House Children's Books, 2021.

Powell, Patricia Hruby. *Lift as you Climb: The Story of Ella Baker.* New York: Simon & Schuster, 2020.

WEBSITES

African American Heroes: Shirley Chisholm
kids.nationalgeographic.com/history/article/shirley-chisholm

Shirley Chisholm
kids.britannica.com/kids/article/Shirley-Chisholm/628650

Women Make History: A Lesson on 20th-Century Activists
civilrightsteaching.org/women-make-history

Philly's 7th Ward
phillys7thward.org/2022/02/shirley-chisholm-black-educator-hall-of-fame-member/

Encyclopedia.com
encyclopedia.com/humanities/encyclopedias-almanacs-transcripts-and-maps/chisholm-shirley-anita

SOURCES

Carol Moseley Braun, senate.gov/senators/FeaturedBios/Featured_Bio_Moseley_Braun.htm

History, Art & Archives, U.S. House of Representatives, "CHISHOLM, Shirley Anita," history.house.gov/People/Listing/C/CHISHOLM,-Shirley-Anita-(C000371)/

Michals, Debra. "Shirley Chisholm." National Women's History Museum. National Women's History Museum, 2015. February 22, 2023., womenshistory.org/education-resources/biographies/shirley-chisholm

Presidential Medal of Freedom, history.com/news/presidential-medal-freedom-truman

ABOUT PLANTING PEOPLE GROWING JUSTICE LEADERSHIP INSTITUTE

Planting People Growing Justice Leadership Institute seeks to plant seeds of social change through education, training, and community outreach.

All proceeds from this book will support the educational programming of Planting People Growing Justice Leadership Institute.